If you can speak...

The Power of Muzik Book

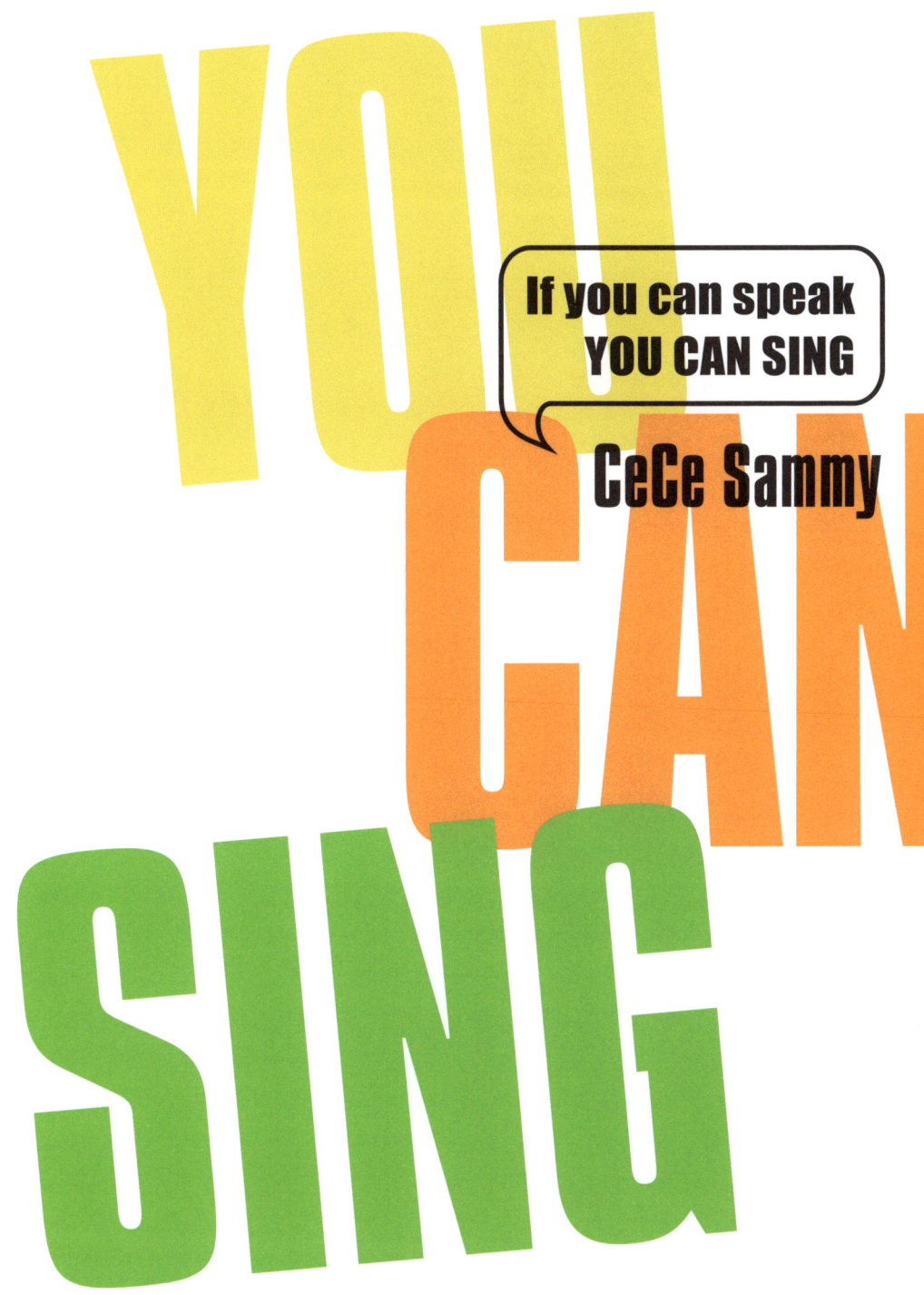

First published in 2019 by Eyewear Publishing Ltd.
Suite 333, 19-21 Crawford Street, Marylebone, London W1H 1PJ

Book design by Malcolm Garrett at Images&Co.
The editor has generally used British spelling in this book.
Printed in England by Pression.

Lyrics reproduced by kind permission of CCA Entertainment.
All photographs reproduced by kind permission of the respective copyright holders.
Thanks to the Coleman family for permission to reproduce the lyrics to *You* (Copyright Control).
Thanks to Charles Michael Duke for permission to use the photograph of him in hospital.

All rights reserved.
Copyright © 2019 Eyewear Publishing Ltd.

www.eyewearpublishing.com
www.powerofmuzik.com

The right of CeCe Sammy to be identified as author of this work has been asserted in accordance with section 77 of the Copyright, Design and Patents Act 1988.

ISBN 978-1-912477-86-9

Contents

	Book Guide	6
	Power of Muzik	8
	Introduction	9
1	**I am ME**	14
2	**Mr Winner vs Mr Failure**	17
3	**Breathing**	30
4	**Dr Disorder**	35
5	**Conflicts! Chaos!**	47
6	**The Unexpected**	54
7	**Vocal Exercises**	54
8	**Fun with *Power of Muzik* Songs**	60
	✱ Fire	61
	✱ Worth It	64
	✱ Shake	66
	✱ Bruised	69
	✱ You	71
	About CeCe Sammy	73

Book Guide

This is my first book about singing and vocal technique, and to accompany the book I've put together an exciting, inspiring multimedia package of recordings and videos to demonstrate what the techniques are and how they can benefit **young people** in so many areas.

Although many of my professional singing clients have found the techniques in this book invaluable, this *first* book is primarily for **secondary school students**, **teachers**, **beginners** and **intermediate singers** as well as for **parents**.

And as well as the science and technique, I've included relevant personal stories and experiences that people of all ages can relate to.

What to expect from the Tasks and Exercises

* Help with projection – speech and singing.
* Help with becoming a better, more confident singer/ performer.
* Help with breathing and breath control in everyday life.
* Help for students focusing on Mathematics, English and studying for exams.
* Help with interviews and public speaking.

What to expect from the Stories

* Overcoming Personal Struggles.
* Managing Negativity and Egos.
* Coping with Conflicts and Chaos.
* Facing the Unexpected.

Accessing the Audio content

 Wherever you see a symbol like this, use your SmartPhone to scan it and link directly to the internet. You'll first need to download a suitable QR code reader App.

In 2018, CeCe Sammy launched a new music therapy initiative called **Power of Muzik**, which empowers and inspires young people going through hard times. *Power of Muzik* uses music therapy techniques and powerful messaging within their music to educate young people, and has worked with the likes of Vanessa Feltz, Ben Ofoedu, Diana Vickers, Mo Jamil and more. As part of the initiative, Sammy formed a collective of singers who have performed at top UK music events throughout 2018. These performances have included the national UK *Steps* tour, *Brighton Pride*, *Fusion Festival* and more. The collective of singers, as well as Sammy and ambassadors for *Power Of Muzik*, have travelled across the UK performing directly to students in their schools.

Introduction

Some years ago I started to make notes for a book that I'd long dreamed of writing; a book about the voice and all its many facets. The anatomy of the voice, the theory of the voice, the vocal chords: how they work, what they do, how we use them and why. My book would include all of this as well as everything I'd learned over the years, not just from school and vocal training but also from some of the incredible writers who had written about this fascinating and versatile thing – the human voice.

As I started writing, the concept for the book began to change and evolve as new and unexpected ideas emerged. I started to ask myself all sorts of questions: not just about the voice in general but also about my personal experiences and what my voice meant to me. I'll admit, the thought of delving into some of this stuff was a little bit scary, but I knew it was something I needed to explore further, so I started writing something that was much more personal to me: not just as a vocal and motivational coach, but also as a mother, a sister, a daughter, and even as a human being. I am someone who, like many people have at times, felt vulnerable, disappointed, disillusioned and hurt. Someone who'd fallen from a great height and almost lost her voice forever… but ultimately I learned to fly again because of that voice.

OK, so some of my questions had answers, but others didn't. This was something that was going to unfold before my eyes. As well as the triumphs that I've experienced I was going to have to look at the failures and the mistakes to get the full picture – because those are the things that make us human and the things we learn from. This was going to be my 'real book' – a book about the power and importance of each and every person's voice: of speech, of singing… and of course music.

Don't get me wrong, the principles, lessons and exercises within this book are vital, but in sharing my personal journey and experiences – not just as a teacher but as a dreamer, a lover of music, its history, and the inner creativity it inspires – I want this to be more than just a book about vocal technique. I want to see confidence and creativity flourish in schools, colleges, hospitals and just about everywhere else. I want to inspire and hopefully educate singers and non-singers to become the next generation of teachers, and I don't just mean the kind of teachers that stand in front of a classroom. We all teach each other without even realising it. In fact, one of my favourite proverbs is, 'As Iron sharpens Iron, so one person sharpens another.' We all have something to learn and something to teach, and my hope is that I can teach you to discover and bring out the voice inside you. Maybe you're discovering it for the first time, or maybe, like me, it's been lost and you need to discover it all over again. Whatever the case, we all have something to say or a song to sing. So I'm making it my mission to make sure everyone is heard. I want to help you to find your voice –

If you can speak, you can sing!

CeCe Sammy

In my *vocal and mind survival guide* I cover four basic subjects:

1. The brain and singing.
2. Singing with habitual response.
3. Recognising when we feel inferior and when we have self-belief.
4. Maintaining balance.

Anyone can do these things, but it's only the dedicated that will find themselves transformed as they're put through their paces. Learning how to sing along with a song, breathing and speak-singing each note is a form of music therapy and it takes hard work, stamina, and sheer determination in its form. Challenges do not come harder than this one, but it's something that can help us right through our lives and in every aspect. So the question is, what are you willing to do to see your life transformed?

Audio – Power of Muzik** song **Fire.
Read the lyrics on page 61.

Power of Muzik *singers*

1
I am ME

In the Learner's dictionary, the phrase 'survival of the fittest' refers to the people or animals who are the strongest and most skilful: able to succeed and to continue to exist. They have 'survival skills'.

In my twenty-five years of working full time in the music and entertainment industry, as well as from my personal experiences, I am convinced that music benefits us all, and furthermore, music can help us with developing our survival skills in a healthy way. A common misconception throughout the world is that the gift of singing is something only certain people have, but the basic truth of the matter is *if you can speak you can sing.* I'm not saying that everyone has the tone of Aretha Franklin, Bruno Mars, Frank Sinatra or Pavarotti, but a tone of a voice is something that we are born with and something we can improve upon, and singing along with a song is something we can all do. It's a truth I've been trying to communicate for years and I'm happy to say that science is now confirming it. In fact, neuropsychologists nod their heads along with philosophers when they say that **music is the natural language of the brain**.

I believe **everyone** has a little bit of that artistic or **creative magic** twinkling away inside; it just reveals itself in different ways in each of us. Of course, there are plenty of professional singers and artists out there, but there are also plenty of people whose creative side reveals itself in the appreciation of what they see, and what they experience, rather than what they do. When you enjoy art, listen to music or go to the theatre and then express thoughts and opinions about what you've seen, that's your creative side bubbling to the surface. You might be commenting on a movie you've enjoyed, recommending a book to a friend, or even cooking for your family.

For example, my seven-year-old daughter loves to watch *Junior MasterChef* with her grandmother – my mother – and she isn't in the least bit shy about expressing her opinion about what she sees. I think that's important. We are all creative people, or, as I like to say, 'lovers of music, art and creativity'. We all have a part in this. The question is, how do you use this creative magic?

The first thing to remember is to look for it **in you**, not just in others.

Task

Right now, I want you to imagine that your life is in show business, as a respected actor or an award-winning singer. There's a mantra I learned when I was very young, and I've adapted it slightly for the purpose of my own work in music. I taught this mantra to many of my famous clients **before** they were famous. Some of them found it a bit silly at the time, but now they tell me that it helped them because they started to believe it, the more and more they did it. One successful client from *The X Factor* told me she repeats it to herself in the mirror before she performs, and has in turn passed it onto other performers.

✳ **Everybody say this aloud now...**

> I AM ME
>
> NOBODY ELSE BUT ME
>
> AND I'D RATHER BE
>
> NOBODY ELSE BUT ME

Repeat this again three times looking at yourself in the mirror. It may seem crazy but it helps explain the next step in my vocal and mind survival guide.

By the way, a nun taught that useful little refrain to me back in Trinidad.

Starting to dream that anything is possible through **Power of Muzik**

2 Mr Winner vs Mr Failure

To help us become winners, the most important raw and basic gift we can give to ourselves is music. Music benefits us all. It affects our emotional development and builds imagination, curiosity, and creative thinking. It can also help people gain or regain their confidence and self-esteem, encouraging them to believe that almost anything is possible.

Youth Empowerment

Music or singing at any level rewires and fixes your brain, which is important because the brain is the organ that nurtures, cares for, protects, and controls everything about us: our thinking, our nature, our doing and our being. Teachers and coaches like me are there to simply guide and educate.

Fact Singing and enjoying or playing music releases feel good hormones into our bodies and can help relieve stress, anxiety and pent up emotions. It can also help us to start believing in ourselves, sending us on a journey of learning and discovery. The trick is not to expect perfection when it comes to learning something new, such as singing. Instead, it's important to realise that achievement and success take time and that the learning, practicing, participating and enjoying are just as important and rewarding as the final results. The results are a lot more satisfying when you work hard during the process, and you'll be surprised how many obstacles you can overcome along the way, and what fears can be conquered just by facing them. Many people in life come to some kind of crossroads. It's a place where you have to make the choice to walk the road of failure or the road of a winner. For every single person I have one thing to say: **listen to music.**

My Story

What if you couldn't communicate with anyone around you? What if you were told you might never speak again? How would you feel if you couldn't sing along with a song you'd always loved? What if you couldn't open your mouth or move your body: unable to ask for water or show facial expressions of any kind? Imagine if you could not remember what day of the week it was or even what year it was. Well, I don't have to imagine any of that stuff because I've experienced it, and it was fear like I'd never known.

I was at a meeting in a restaurant, not feeling well. It was nothing specific, but I was sweating and I knew something was wrong. As time passed I was finding it more and more difficult to speak, and then I just passed out completely. The next thing I remember was lying down on a bed with people standing over me. A doctor kept asking, 'can you say your name? Do you know what year we are in?'

I started panicking because I couldn't speak, and I **didn't** know my name or what year I was in. It was the worst feeling

I've ever experienced - very scary. The only thing I could grab onto was the fact that I could hear my sister's voice, and I could also hear the voice of the client who I'd been in a meeting with. Those two voices I recognized. Other than that, everything was a complete blank. I felt like I was in the middle of nothing. And I then passed out again.

When I finally woke again a few days later, I couldn't speak or even open my eyes. I started trying to move my finger as if to say, 'I'm here!' But even a tiny movement was impossible.

I'd suffered a brain aneurysm and for a while I couldn't even breathe properly on my own, so I had tubes up my nose and down my throat to keep everything going. When the tubes came out I started to panic, but I concentrated hard on my breathing until it started to become normal. Over the next few weeks, I couldn't do anything for myself. I had to be showered, fed and tended to in every way. It was very demeaning. Luckily, my sister was there to take over when it came to bathing and showering, but I had to be wheeled to the bathroom in a chair and transferred to another chair while she washed me. I couldn't do a thing for myself.

Everyone spoke to me as though I was a very old deaf person, but I wanted to be able to tell the doctors and nurses, 'I can hear you; I can do this.' My sister, however, continued to speak to me in a normal voice, and she also played music that she knew I liked and that would stimulate me. She played specific classical pieces, as well as gospel music, which gave me strength, and as it played I would move my fingers, pretending I was playing the piano.

I kept moving my fingers, day and night, just like I was playing a scale, and once I'd mastered that I started making the sounds that I make in my vocal exercises: the 'goo' and the 'gee' sounds. It was exhausting but I did it every day, as I got stronger and stronger.

Eventually I could get up, but I still couldn't move the whole of my right side for a while, so I told myself to take one step at a time. I took each step in rhythm with the vocal exercises – one step for each sound – and that really helped focus me and speed up my progress. When a speech therapist came to see me, she was very impressed to see how the vocal exercises had helped not only my speech but my body function as well.

I'm not saying any of this was easy. It was often very boring and frustrating because I could only do so much at any one time, but I kept focusing on it because I didn't want to be flat on my back, relying on other people for the rest of my life.

The thing I want to make very clear is that none of this recovery happened because I'm better or even stronger than anyone else. I was in a very dark place, distraught and crying as I tried my best to move and speak. What made a difference was that I didn't stop. I kept that repetition going. If I had stopped, I might not have progressed as I did or fully recovered, but I was determined to be able to speak again and to fully pronounce my words to say things such as 'a cup was a cup', 'please give me a smile', or to be able to make my right foot move again. I could not say the difference between 'h' or 'she' when I was able to form a word at first as I could only say 'he'. I was determined to take that one step and then be proud of myself for doing it, and even more so for believing in myself.

Even now, years later, I have flashbacks, remembering that I was unable to do so many basic, ordinary things which, up until then, I had completely taken for granted.

In my story, Mr Failure and Mr Winner both stood in front of me, looking me in the eye and willing me to make a decision. It was up to me whose team I chose to be on; nobody else could decide for me. Thankfully, I chose to be on the side of Mr Winner, even though at times it seemed impossible that I could win.

So for all of you who are going through bad times or experiencing pain, whether that pain is physical or perhaps a painful thought or memory, I want you to do everything you can to **find your voice**. Learn or re-learn how to **speak your words** and **sing your song**. Just like I did.

Task

* Can you think of a time when music helped you through a difficult time?
  Write it down, think about it and remember how it helped.

  _____

* If you cannot think of a time when music helped you through a difficult time, think of a song that simply made you happy, or want to sing or dance.
  For example, when I am feeling tired or low or need a bit of inspiration, I often listen to the soundtrack to the movie Inception *by Hans Zimmer, which takes me through many different emotions.*

* When you think of that song, celebrate in your mind that music was there for you. Music was your friend, whether you were happy or sad.

Write down the answers to these questions

If you do not have an answer to some of these questions, don't worry. Just come back another time and try it again.

[Also, write everything in pencil rather than pen because in a few months you might want to change your answers, and that is fine!]

✷ What style of music do you most enjoy listening to?
Tick the box or boxes you enjoy.

Pop ☐   Rock ☐   Musicals ☐   Jazz ☐   Dance ☐
Country ☐   Alternative ☐   Hip-hop ☐   Grime ☐
Classical ☐   *Something else? Write down your choices.*

_____

*It might not necessarily be what your friends like, but that doesn't matter. Write down the genre or genres **you** like.*

✷ What songs do you most enjoy singing along to?

_____

✷ Are there some genres of music that you play more frequently at certain times? For example: do you play one kind of music when you're happy and another when you're sad? If that is the case, write it down and don't feel embarrassed about your answers. You are the only person who will see this and it will help you to learn more about yourself.

_____

✱ Which artists inspire you musically?

_____

_____

_____

✱ Which actors or actresses do you admire or enjoy watching?

_____

_____

_____

✱ Is there a performer that you enjoy imitating or that you aspire to sound or be like? If so, who is it?

_____

✱ After you write down your answers to **all** these questions, take the time to think about the reasons **why** you might enjoy a certain style of music or **why** you like certain artists or performers. How do they make you feel? Think of three adjectives that describe how a certain song makes you feel.

_____

_____

_____

Exercise

Here's something you should do regularly...

* Choose a song you really love.
* Listen to it – close your eyes and **really listen to it**.
* As you listen, hum along to it. Sing with it gently. Relax your neck and shoulders while you listen.
* Now immerse yourself completely in the song with a smile on your face – **even if you don't feel like smiling at the time.**

Note *You can try this again with more technical know-how once you've completed the vocal exercises a few times, but for now, just hum along with it and sing gently – only going as high or as low you can go without straining. Keep your face relaxed.*

Exercise

Breathing in through your nose
AND ***breathing out though your nose.***

- ✸ Imagine a balloon as you are breathing in from a low, deep place. Allow yourself to feel your stomach getting bigger like a balloon when you breathe in. This is the RIGHT way.
- ✸ Start to control your breathing in (inhaling) through your nose slowly, counting to four as you do this.

    As you are breathing in, put your hand on your stomach by your belly, and make sure that you keep your shoulders relaxed.
- ✸ Hold your breath for two seconds after you breathe in before blowing out (exhaling) through your nose slowly. Count to four again as you exhale.
- ✸ Imagine a balloon again. As you're breathing out, you should feel what happens to a balloon that is losing air – your stomach should get smaller.

Try this again, it may take time to get it right but repeat and try...

1. Breathe in from a lower place (lower end of your stomach not upper end).
2. Feel your stomach getting bigger like a balloon, but keep your shoulders relaxed.
3. Breathe out and feel your stomach getting smaller as you breathe out.

This helps you to take control of your body and your body will realise that you are in charge.

This is a lot of information where you are doing many things at the same time and being fully aware of what you are doing.

INHALING and counting to 4 as you are breathing in, then HOLDING your breath for two seconds before blowing out and EXHALING through your nose slowly, counting to four again as you exhale.

*Please note that most people breathe in from their chest when singing or giving a speech, which is WRONG as they are taking a shallow breath. With lots of RIGHT practice, **you will** start to do this.*

Every time you do this, write this down with a pencil as you ask yourself a repeated question...

Questions

* Today, do you feel your stomach becoming like a balloon and it gets bigger when you breathe in?

  Tick the box ☐

* Today, when you breathe out, your stomach should get smaller like a balloon losing air.

  Tick the box ☐

As you get better at doing the exercise for a few weeks or a few months, you can make the out-breaths longer.

Try counting to six or eight as you are exhaling. I've been doing it for so long that I practice counting to twelve or sometimes sixteen, but it's taken me years to get to that.

Now let's move on to breathing in through your nose, pursing your lips and ***breathing out through your mouth.***

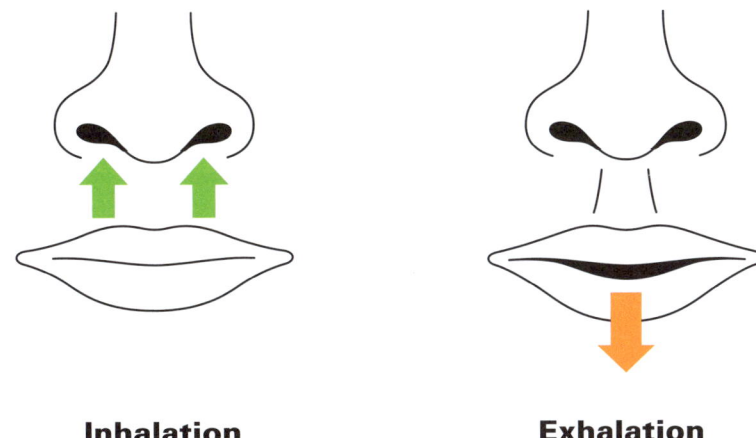

Inhalation   **Exhalation**

- Now Inhale through your nose and count to four.
- Hold your breath for two, and then purse your lips and exhale *through your **mouth***. Count as you breathe out slowly, making the breath as long as you can, naturally.

Breathing in and out though your nose is used in most yoga practices, and breathing out through the mouth is what singers do. I think it's important to practice both ways of breathing. Exhaling through your nose is the most natural way to breathe and assists with mindful practices like yoga, but exhaling through the mouth helps vocal control as well as lung capacity.

Our body is all connected and we have to find balance, which gives us an anchor. I'll explore breathing more in the next chapter, but for now let's concentrate on the calming, focused decision to listen to music differently.

The above exercise will naturally bring a sense of calm to take you to a place of well-being. Natural breathing is the beginning of your journey and where you start to let those good hormones into your body and into your life.

After giving you lots of information, I have a story for you...

Luena's Story
A shy girl who became a pop star

Luena is a nineteen-year-old singer who appeared on *The X Factor* in 2016, but before she became the confident singer that people saw on TV, she was a young girl fighting depression and having problems at school.

Being a mixed-race girl, Luena felt like she didn't fit in: Was she black? Was she white? She didn't have many friends and was never invited to her classmates' parties or even to hang out. In Luena's mind it was because of her dual heritage and those negative thoughts quickly turned into low self-esteem and depression.

When Luena started singing, it was for herself more than anyone else. After a while she started to feel more confident and eventually she felt brave enough to enter singing competitions, which encouraged her to take chances. After working with her for quite some time, I saw how much her confidence had grown and encouraged her to audition for *The X Factor*. However, I wanted her to realise that it wasn't just about beating the rest of the competition; it was about how she viewed herself. Ultimately, she faced Mr Failure and triumphed. She chose Mr Winner. She chose to take the chance no matter what the outcome. She might not have won *The X Factor* but she learned the skill of trying again and

@LuenaOfficial

again with a smile on her face. Since then she's performed in public, been a TV judge, and even worked alongside some famous pop stars – opening for *Steps* on their UK tour and performing at *Fusion Festival* in 2018.

Now you've read my story and Luena's. What's yours? And what choices will you make to affect the outcome?

Audio *– Luena Official song **Worth It**.*
Listen to her voice sounding confident and secure in herself.
Read the lyrics on page 64.

3 Breathing

Unless we have health problems or have particularly bad posture, most of us don't really have to work at breathing. There are no special exercises necessary for strengthening our regular breathing muscles, so unless a doctor says differently, they're fine doing their job just as they are. The diaphragm's function as the main breathing muscle is to make room for the lungs to expand and fill with air, and because it's an involuntary muscle, we naturally don't fight against it.

When we sing, however, we need to regulate the rate at which we take the air in, and we also need to regulate the rate at which we expel the air from our lungs. It's here that other muscles help to regulate the process of breathing: the ribcage and abdominal muscles for instance. The trick is to keep this action of breathing as natural as possible when you sing; just as natural as it is when you speak. A good singing teacher should be very specific when explaining or demonstrating breathing to a singing student, so it doesn't end up in a kind of panic attack, where the singer feels like their breath control is lost. At the same time, singers should know that it takes time to understand breathing points and the exercise below is important for focus and for transformation, in your speech as well as your singing.

This type of strict focus on breathing also applies directly to students in their approach to English, Mathematics and preparing for exams. When students get low marks or feel they're struggling or making mistakes, they can adopt and practice this method of natural breathing, helping them to **live in the present**, to focus and to try again.

I have met and worked with teenagers studying for important exams, who learned how to better communicate with teachers and their fellow students, and learned to cope with and enjoy some of the classes and subjects they had previously struggled in.

For example, teenager Denis Coleman had an intense one-to-one French class. In learning the breathing exercises, he was able to calm down and concentrate on his memory and pronunciation during his French oral exam. Many of the exercises in the class were oral. Breathing exercises were the key to help his nerves. *This can help you too!*

Denis Coleman

Example

I recently worked on a new BBC TV show doing something that was a world away from coaching on a TV talent show. On the show, I worked with a twenty-three-year-old guy, Charles, who recently had a double lung transplant due to an illness he'd had since he was five. He always loved music and had a dream of singing publicly, but because he had been waiting for new lungs for so long, often isolated in hospital, this seemed like an impossible dream.

The idea was that by the end of the TV show, with coaching, he'd be able to perform a song with a choir, proving to himself and others that he could do it, despite the mental and physical barriers.

Some of the things I had him do during our time together were probably the complete opposite of what other coaches might have done, but to me overcoming something like

Charles Michael Duke rehearsing with CeCe (courtesy BBC)

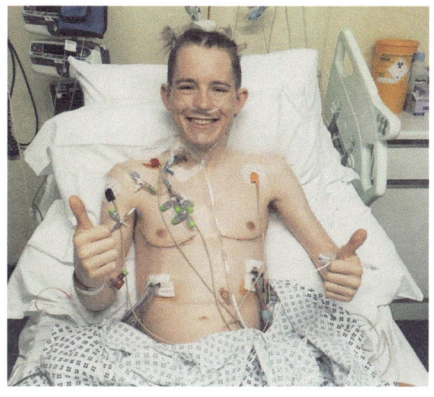
Charles Michael Duke

that starts in the mind – not the body. He already had a very lively personality and I strongly believed that his positive attitude had helped him massively during tough times. But he'd been struggling to breathe for so long, it had become the norm, so now he had to learn how to breathe naturally, making full use of his new lungs. He was literally re-learning to do something that we all do thousands of times a day without even thinking.

So instead of just standing around a piano doing the vocal exercises, I gave him vocal homework where he had to do the exercises while going up and down stairs and even walking and jogging on the beach with me. At the end of the show, he performed with a choir in front of his mother and girlfriend.

My Story

One day during my illness while I was lying in my hospital bed, I listened to some music. This was after weeks of tears and silent panic each time the lights went out and I was left alone with nothing but the sound of my own beating heart. It was a real step forward. That day, I immersed myself in the music and focused on controlling my breathing. Then I clearly envisaged myself walking and talking. I wasn't wishing that it might happen, I was actually telling myself that it was happening.

Work on controlling your breathing **every day** – *No skipping!*

Summary of Chapters 2 and 3

In these chapters I've given examples of training your mindset and shown you breathing exercises that will help you to take control of your mind and body. Make a note of what you've learned – write it down and keep coming back to it. You may be able to help others with what you've learned.

*Audio – **Power Of Muzik** song **Shake**.*
Read the lyrics on page 66.

*You will read that they shake themselves and dance no matter what happens, taking control of their minds and bodies. Well-known singer **DJ Sonique** starts to sing the first verse, then a singing teacher Wendy Sheppard sings the second verse and in all of the choruses are teenagers and young people singing with them including a 16-year-old rapper **Reece**.*

ENJOY and dance!

Angel** (14) and **Reece** (16) sing and rap in the song **Shake

4 Dr Disorder

Sometimes, a kind of **thinking disorder** causes us to focus on things that can distort what we see and what we hear: our own voices, other people's voices, even how we view our bodies and our lives. As a vocal coach, I meet singers all the time, and one of the things I always tell them is, '**never shy away from letting your voice be heard because you feel you're not as good as other people**.' You'll gain tremendous experience by singing – by yourself and also with other people. With time, you'll develop your skill and hopefully start to see your voice as an instrument.

Even if you don't consider yourself a natural singer, the action of singing can be just as useful and important, helping to build inner strength and giving you the tools to communicate with others with confidence. It might be a strength that you never even knew you had, but trust me you were born with it.

Sai's Story

Sai was an Indian guy of about twenty-three who worked with computer technology and was good at his job. But in that job, Sai was quite isolated, and that's where the problem was. Sai found it extremely hard to communicate with other people. In fact, even having friends was hard for Sai because he was so insular and his solitary work environment wasn't helping. He also longed to have a girlfriend but just didn't have the confidence to talk to women. When Sai came to me, it wasn't to learn how to sing, it was more about music helping him to focus. This was a learning experience for me too as it was the first time I'd worked with someone who needed to learn something other than singing.

He started off with a very negative attitude to himself and his ability to communicate. He'd convinced himself that he wasn't popular and that people wouldn't like him. The exercises and coaching I gave him helped him change that distorted way of thinking. Through those repeated exercises and through the discipline of learning songs and performing, he was able to be much more coherent when he spoke.

Eventually, his confidence was such that he had the courage to join a dating website and go on dates. His confidence grew as he accepted that he didn't have to be the most popular person in the world, he just had to be comfortable in his own skin.

Asher's Story
A boy who was bullied at school but then became a confident speaker

Asher was 16 when we met, and another example of somebody who used music as a way to build confidence. Asher loved music but again, he found it impossible to engage in a conversation with people. He was worried that he wasn't cool or interesting enough and had become very isolated. Much of this came out of the bad experience he'd had at school in the shape of bullying. When I first met him, his shoulders were slumped, he looked down all the time and he didn't look at other people. He certainly did not talk about how he felt, and when he did speak, he'd over-think and worry what he should or shouldn't say. He also had issues about his weight and low self-esteem. He had been in a situation where he was physically bullied and would hide in cupboards at school so people could not find him.

Asher used my vocal exercises as a way to escape from the horrible situation that he was in. As he did the exercises and started to sing thinking of the lyrics, he was able to become different characters, almost as though he was acting out a role. In that way music was taking him out of his introverted self and showing him other possibilities – of how he could be without all that negativity.

Asher is now 21, and in great demand as a spokesperson for a major anti-bullying campaign in schools all over the UK. He performs his songs and talks about his experiences of being bullied, and how music helped him to overcome his low self-esteem and get involved with the anti-bullying music campaign.

That's what I mean when I say that music is for everyone, because we can use it as an anchor to centre and ground us. With Asher I had no idea whether he'd be able to overcome those deep-rooted self-esteem issues, but when I look at him today, I see a complete transformation. Asher is so much more confident and knows what he wants and is not afraid to express it.

Asher Knight

Audio – Power of Muzik song **Bruised**.
Listen to the lyrics on page 69.

The lyrics are very vulnerable when a young boy **Michael Rice**, who won the BBC TV show *All Together Now*, sings the song. **Asher Knight** and **Luena Martinez** and a school choir join in later in the song. They all combine to show people that singing a vulnerable song can help you to share with other people.

Vocal technique is the next basic foundation of the voice, whether we are speaking or singing. I've studied many different vocal techniques and many of them have something valid to teach us, but I would suggest caution if you meet a teacher or coach who only teaches what works for them. Their technique might not be applicable to you and that's when feelings of failure tend to set in.

The important thing to remember is that we are all different and we're all working at different levels. A familiar foe I like to call Dr Disorder often rears his ugly head when we judge ourselves harshly or talk negatively to ourselves about ourselves. Dr Disorder is the inner critical voice who can easily take us over if we let him. He can take away our energy, our confidence and our self-esteem, but there are many ways to combat him.

I was never as good as my sister was with finances and wasted lots as a child. Give me five pounds and I'd spend ten pounds. Give my sister five pounds and she will save half of it instinctively. That being said, I'm now in a position where I can provide for my family and friends and for myself. In the past, I had friends and acquaintances who would tell me that I was making the wrong choices and making bad business decisions, and my determination to prove them wrong turned me into a woman who built a business which made deals for hundreds of thousands of pounds, and also I have been a key part of TV shows costing millions.

My Story

I learned about how Dr Disorder can disrupt your life from a young age but I was lucky enough to have the guidance of a strong mother. My sister was always seen as the academic one and I was seen as the creative one, but while our mother encouraged those strengths in us and accepted us in our different ways of learning, she also made sure that we nurtured both aspects of our character, which she knew would develop and come in useful as we got older. My mother showed me when I was a child that she trusted me to buy some of the things I needed by giving me a certain amount of money and letting me decide how best to spend it wisely, but she would also tell me how much change she expected to see from the amount she'd given me. I failed that task many times, but as I grew up and saw the repercussions of not having enough money, I started to pay more attention to budgeting and finance.

My mother with me when I was a little girl

My mother also made me sit down and work hard at my Maths, which she knew was not my strong subject. On one occasion I got a very low marks in my Maths class and I felt like I would never master the subject or be as strong as I was in English and History. My mother helped me realise that I simply needed to spend more time and focus on Maths despite how much it scared me. At the same time, my sister did not want to play the piano because that was seen as my instrument and she didn't want to be compared to me, so my mother told her to choose a different instrument to keep her creative flame flickering. She chose the violin. Although my sister ended up working in the finance world, she's recently started working on contracts and finance for big budget movies, where her creative side has really come into its own.

Me with Frank DiLeo (Michael Jackson's manager)

As an adult, I worked with Frank DiLeo, who was Michael Jackson's manager. He was someone in the music industry who helped me see the power of positive thinking and of focus and told me that one of the keys to gaining strength and confidence was to learn how to embrace my mistakes, rather than letting them overwhelm me. He would call me into breakfast meetings before we started our day, always reminding me not to be afraid of trying new things and to see myself as an entrepreneur. He saw me as a risk-taker, and a leader, which he felt was a good thing as long as I didn't let my mistakes drag me down. He also taught me to understand the difference between real friends and acquaintances. Frank was like the father I never had, and both he and my mother were a big influence on the way I thought about myself, always striving to embrace the positive and to push away the negative clutches of Dr Disorder.

**My top tip for youth empowerment is vocal technique
– fight your thinking disorders!**

There's a lot of pressure on young people today: a pressure to be or look a certain way or have certain material things. Advertising and social media help fuel it, giving Dr Disorder the power to leave many young people feeling like they're not good enough or they don't fit in. It may be to do with body image or a popularity issue, but it's something we all need to address. A person who doesn't have the physique of a catwalk model might be a wonderful singer, another person who can't kick a ball straight might be destined to help or teach others. We **all** need to fight this thinking disorder that tells us we're not good enough and focus on what we **can** do – which is pretty much anything.

This is where vocal technique comes into its own. I strongly believe that vocal technique should be repetitious. Yes, repetition can be boring at times but it's important to understand that repetition gives us a foundation of discipline and survival for every area of our lives. Repetition also helps us to maintain our voice, which will continually change and develop as we get older. Our technique is something that should become habitual like:

* Brushing our teeth
* Showering
* Changing our clothes

A Habitual Response

Habitual means a way of behaving that is well-established or persistent. A **response** is a reaction to something. So a **habitual response** is the way in which somebody would usually react to something. Now this might be a good or bad thing, depending on the person, and also what they're reacting to and how. In the case of the right vocal technique, a habitual response is **definitely** a good thing because habit encourages discipline, which works for people of all ages and ability.

Allow vocal technique to become a necessity in your life – to warm up your voice and exercise your vocal cords. But let's not stop there! Let's learn how to translate vocal technique into an actual place of singing a song, performing a whole show, being a confident person when speaking publicly, or even holding your own at a party or even just hanging out with friends.

Why do you brush your teeth every day or wash or take a shower? Because it's one of life's necessities, right? True, it won't kill you if you don't, but nobody wants to look dirty and have smelly breath and bad teeth. This is why these actions become a habit: something that's learned at a young age and repeated throughout life.

Teachers and Parents Think about small children. If a child sees an action repeated often enough they'll learn and copy that action. These habits can be good or bad, so it's important that we make sure we nurture helpful, positive and healthy habits.

Example

Having targets and goals are important because they help us focus on the good things about ourselves. So if you set yourself short-term targets every day (things you'd like to achieve or accomplish on a particular day) and write down long-term goals (things you're working towards achieving) your habitual response to yourself and what you do will be positive and healthy – no matter what anybody else says. In the same way, if we tell ourselves the same negative stuff over and over again, we start to believe it is a fact and then act accordingly. That's definitely not healthy.

Exercise

Let's apply habitual response while singing...

Audio – Youth Empowerment.

In this exercise, my **Power Of Muzik** singers of different ages teach different versions of the song *The Tide Is High*.

* **Luena** *speaks and guides everyone as another singer is singing the lead. Luena sings on the ends of the lines a bit louder so you can sing in those exact places with her.*
* **Angel who is 14** *– She sings the lead vocal. Listen to her but then also join in with her.*
* **Denis who is 15** *– His voice has not broken so try imitating his voice and see what he does at the ends of the lines. Boys: follow Denis and let him teach you.*
* **Dan in his early 20s** *will show you how to sing when your voice has broken and is much lower.*

Audio – *A personal vocal coaching session with me on a song called* **Try A Little Tenderness***.*

Listen to the full version where I talk to my **Power Of Muzik** *singers and you will hear my notes to them.*
Then try singing with the backing track where I will talk to you.
Be brave and sing!

Doing warm-up exercises with Asher, Denis, Angel and Luena

My Tip

❋ When you're practicing a song, it's important not to sing the whole song straight through without stopping.

❋ Instead, stop at the end of each line and tackle any specific area that you feel you need to focus on.
   Repeat, stop, repeat, stop, and repeat – until you have mastered it.

❋ Stop and repeat until you feel you've mastered each exercise.

❋ Learn to distinguish between songs that truly suit your voice as opposed to songs that you like. Of course, sometimes it can be both but that isn't always the case. Your favourite track might not be the best song for you to sing. I'm not saying that you shouldn't experiment and have fun.
   Experimentation is vital and exciting, but it's important to understand the facets of your unique voice

and how to shape the sound of it.

❋ Regular vocal technique during song rehearsal is important. This rule also applies when you're warming up your voice.

Task

❋ Try recording your voice, then listen back to it and judge yourself in an honest but encouraging way.

If it doesn't sound as good as you imagined it, don't feel defeated. Celebrate the things you do like about it and then set about trying to correct the things that you don't. Try not to let negative thoughts and emotions get in the way of learning and growing.

In summary, vocal technique will naturally lead you to self-improvement. You'll dig deep inside yourself and discover things about yourself you didn't even know were in there and that will eventually shine through in a confident performance – whether that's singing or expressing yourself with your voice in some other way. No more Dr Disorder.

No more Dr Disorder

5 Conflict! Chaos!

Most people will experience feelings of inferiority in their lives: at school, college or work. This is certainly true of people who are in the arts (actors, writers, singers, dancers, etc.) because they're literally putting themselves out there to be judged by anyone who sees, hears, reads or criticizes their work. I've also met plenty of singers who spend far too much time comparing themselves to other singers, and who end up feeling inferior. It's an easy habit to slip into, so how we tackle the situation is very important.

If you start comparing yourself unfavourably to somebody else, try to recognize what's happening and stop. Understand that this is a vulnerability that most artists experience, and try not to let these kinds of thoughts and emotions recur without addressing them.

Stop

See these feelings for what they really are: **conflict and chaos, drama, and ego!**

Resisting your feelings of inferiority will help you become a well-rounded singer or speaker, but understanding your natural vulnerabilities will help build a much-needed strength in you. As a performer, or even as a human being, you are bound to experience rejection somewhere along the way, and it's important to realise that these disappointments and knock-backs are just part of life and can actually help to build strength and resilience. Accepting this, and keeping an open heart and mind to whatever comes your way will lead you to becoming a more well-rounded performer… and a well-rounded person.

Auditions, Exams, Results

Attending auditions can be a nerve-wracking experience, similar to when students in their last year of school are waiting for their exam results. Experiences like this can lead us to develop feelings of inferiority because we are often going up against others of similar talent or perhaps students who are always getting top marks. The important thing to remember with auditions, exams and results, is that it's you who must make the decision to believe in yourself.

In **auditions** remember that **your** talents and abilities are not defined by somebody else's choice for a particular part or role.

During **study** and **exams** remember that **you** must learn to find the best way forward if you begin to feel overwhelmed, and dictate the speed at which you go.

*Audio – **You** is a song that 15-year-old **Denis Coleman** wrote. Read the lyrics on page 71.*

Music is like a diary for Denis as he confesses a journey that he is on. An early stage of a friendship and relationship – the unnecessary drama that begins by uncertainty. As well as relationships and friendships, there is the fear of drama during exams and over-thinking about what the teachers really want but you feel you cannot tell. The lyrics will relate to all secondary students in one way or another.

In the world of Music Television there are so many factors as to why someone might make it (or not) through the first few rounds of a talent show. It might not just be with their voice; instead it could be their character, their background, even the style of music they're performing. Maybe the TV show already has too much of the same thing. It doesn't mean that all the people who don't get through don't have talent. It just means that they are not right for **that** show at **that** time or maybe the producers can see talent in them but feel they might need a little more practice or time to develop their craft. The same applies to the students in that difficult final year waiting for their results. Whatever happens, know that you must take the time to learn and achieve at your own pace. If you have to re-sit an exam, it's not the end of the world.

I've worked on so many music TV shows: *The Voice, The X Factor, All Together Now*, plus casting on *American Idol, America's Got Talent* as well as other major TV events and even movies. So I've listed here some practical tips for auditioning. These tips don't just apply to singers either. Most of them could be applied to people interviewing for college or a job, or standing up in front of the classroom to deliver a report.

Remember

1. The audition or interview starts the minute you walk through the door. Be aware of your posture, expressions and attitude from the beginning right up to the end.

2. When you're singing a song in audition (or reciting a speech or monologue) think of yourself as a storyteller and make it your own. Singing is just like speaking when you're telling a dramatic story. You don't tell that story all

in one tone, do you? There are natural rises and falls, highs and lows in the voice when we tell a story or engage in a conversation. Think about that when you deliver the lyrics of the song or the words of the speech.

3 If you make a mistake, shake it off immediately and finish the performance. Don't stay in that moment. The audience (or judges) will be more forgiving if they see that you carried on despite your slip up. In fact, if you are really slick about it, they might not even notice the mistake at all.

4 Many people will be nervous at an audition or a presentation involving other students or teachers, however well-prepared they are, so here are some **basic practical tips** on how to combat and overcome nerves and those annoying physical manifestations that those nerves can cause. **Sweaty hands**: If your hands feel sweaty and clammy, shake your hands free. **Uptight shoulders**: Some people find that their shoulders start to get all uptight when nerves kick in. This often happens when people are over-thinking an audition or interview or are maybe trying a little too hard to please. Be aware of this: relax your shoulders and breathe in and out naturally. **Wobbly legs**: If you feel your legs are shaking with nerves before an audition, repeat to yourself, 'I am strong'. As you are saying it, keep breathing in deeply and breathing out. Try to distract yourself by your focused exercises. **Shifty eyes**: Letting your eyes dart nervously around the room can make others sense your anxiety and make them feel uncomfortable. As you speak or sing, try to keep a gentle fixed gaze for a while. Be aware of your eyes and try to keep their movement as natural as possible.

5 Take every opportunity to try out for different things. The

more experience you have performing, speaking and writing the more you will improve your performance. If you sing in front of people enough times you will:

* Face your fears
* Learn from your mistakes
* Test the waters for public feedback

Experience

I have worked with many successful artists at the beginning of their careers and one of the key elements to their success is that they have learned how to handle their nerves when performing for an audience – their nerves are hidden or cleverly camouflaged. I've seen mega-famous artists who get so nervous before a performance, they vomit before they go on stage – but they get over it!

One of the biggest tasks in an audition is to believe in yourself no matter what happens.

Continual growth is important.

Task

Have you been in an audition before? Have you performed as a singer or have you spoken or read something in public? Try to remember the feelings that you had inside when you did it. Whether those feelings were bad or good or you had no feeling either way. Now simply breathe in and out - as you are about to try a new kind of audition, and a new kind of exam.

1. Find two songs on your phone, tablet or computer: one fast or mid-tempo and another which is slow. The tracks must

have the singer on it as you are now going to be an actor / actress and perform them.

2 Perform two versions. First a deliberately **extroverted performance: over the top and confident**, and then a deliberately **introverted performance: shy and understated**.

3 Do this with both songs, singing along with the vocal. One after the other.

4 Now do the same songs again in the same introverted / extroverted style, this time **speaking** the lyrics rather than singing them, **but** taking the breath points as you would if you were singing them.

*Audio – 15-year-old **Denis Coleman** sings his song **You** in two versions – an extroverted performance and then an introverted performance of the same song.*
Read the lyrics on page 71.

5 When you have chosen your song and you are finished, close your eyes and be honest with yourself. Which performance of each **spoken** song did you prefer and feel more comfortable with? The introverted or the extroverted?

6 Now repeat the version you liked *less*, again **speaking** the lyric. Face that fear. Focus and remember your mindset should be about overcoming that fear.

7 Even though you are doing the song you liked less, you are instilling the notion in yourself that you are **always ready** and **always prepared for change**.

CeCe Sammy

6 The Unexpected

What is the course of your life? Where are you going? Where are you heading? Let your creative dreams live daily and let your imagination flow so they become **actual intentions**. It can sometimes be a struggle to believe in ourselves, no matter how much we try. The personal stories in this book – from my near-death experience to people facing their fears of low self-esteem, overcoming being bullied and concern at certain school subjects – show us that we all have an inner strength and we can walk our own paths. We have a choice. You have a choice.

Leeds College of Music is a leading conservatoire of music, an educational institution that I have great respect for, and a place where I love to give masterclasses. In an article I wrote for their *Musicians Survival Guide* I wrote: 'Don't wait until you go on stage to figure out what you're going to do. Many people come to me and say that they will wait until they are on stage, as the adrenaline will help to give a better performance. In my experience this is not a good idea.'

Of course your adrenaline may well kick-in in the heat of the moment, while performing or doing an audition or sitting an exam… but it might not! If you spend time on you, giving yourself the right tools and the time to learn, imagine the possibilities. You will have all that creative magic on your side, whether you're a singer, actor, performer or a student of any kind.

Most of those A-list, big-time singers and actors were people that rehearsed, rehearsed and then rehearsed some more. They had goals to achieve and I want **you** to think about your goals and then work towards them. Repetition and rehearsal will often seem tedious but it's that focus and dedication to whatever you've chosen to do that is vital if you want to be a success in your chosen field.

You are the next wave of change and I encourage you to reach for your goals. I want to make sure you know that **anything is possible** and that you can be the next **A-Lister**!

As I've said throughout this book, chaos, conflict and drama are all around us, and we all have egos to keep in check, but I want you to embrace **the unexpected**. Let things you thought were impossible become possible. Music education and understanding can help everyone in every area of life so take your steps, one by one, and find your voice.

Remember – *if you can speak you can sing!*

7 Vocal Exercises

Audio – *Various vocal Warm-Up Exercises can always be found on the **Power of Muzik** website.*

There are many different vocal technique exercises, but one of the things they have in common is that they teach us how to understand vowels and consonants.

Exercise 1 – **Vowels**

In the English language we use the vowels **A, E, I, O, U**

- Say **A** – now say *AH*
- Say **E** – now say *EH*
- Say **I** – now say *E*
- Say **O** – now say *OH*
- Say **U** – now say *OO*

Exercise 2 – **Consonants**

B, C, D, F, G, H, J, K, L, M, N, P, Q, R, S, T, V, W, X, Y, Z

Find two different words from each of these consonant letters. For example, **B** – say *BEE* then say *BAT*

Consonants can be spoken and sung in a subtle way or in a

powerful way according to the word and in the context.

Now as you say the words again in **B** – pronounce *BAT* with a hard **B**, then go harder on the **T**.

This is the basic part of warming-up your voice. Keep adjusting it and change according to the vocal with music on.

The vocal warm-up technique boot-camp exercises will help you with repetition – how to stop, repeat, stop, repeat, which you can put into practice when studying or doing homework.

Warming-up your voice and preparing your mindset is vital

* Start as low as you can and go as high as you're able to do without hurting your voice.

* Hit each note. As you get higher, drop the jaw and relax.

* Keep breathing and relax your shoulders.

* Think about how you use your voice at different times during the day. For instance, you'll generally use the lower part of your voice first thing in the morning when you wake up. Then as the day goes on, the range will expand to include the mid and upper ranges.
   When you get excited or more expressive, you'll often use the higher part of your voice. Notice that during all this, you never stop to think about how high or how low you are speaking. You don't suddenly think, I have to stop because my voice is going too high or too low. Am I right? You just do it without thinking, using your voice in a natural way.

* Well, it should be just the same with singing, which is why you need to warm-up all areas of your voice before you sing.

* I often tell students to smile while they are singing, because it brightens the sound and helps to keep them in tune. This doesn't just apply to the higher notes, but to the lower ones too.

* When you start to feel a change in your voice, as you get higher, (like a break or a crack) start to drop your jaw as you prepare yourself to hit those higher notes but don't try to sing louder. Each note is different and feels different.

* Vowels and consonants are equally important when performing a song, so make sure you incorporate both during your warm-up.

* The difference between speaking and singing is that the vowel sounds often change when we sing. Vowels can be lengthened and changed, depending on the style, rhythm and timing of the song.

The habitual response teaches you focus, but vocal exercise will help with sudden changes. Please note that even coaches like myself make mistakes when we are warming up, so don't stop if you make a mistake, just go over it again. Let your mistakes shine a light on the exercises (or parts of an exercise) that you need to practice or repeat.

Remember

A sports player does not just get on the field – they have to warm up their muscles.

In the same way, singers (and even non-singers) should warm up their voices, so please make sure you do it before you start to rehearse your song or begin your day. Protect your voice and **have fun**.

Vocal exercises are important, and they're not just about proving you can sing or reach the high notes. Done in the right way they can be like a form of meditation – calming the mind. They can bring tranquility and help you stay free of distraction.

*James CC (one of the **Power of Muzik** singers) is teaching vocal exercises at the schools as he learnt them from CeCe – it is not about being a pop star. It is about learning how to focus when doing subjects like Maths where you feel confused. Vocal exercises teach focus*

8 Fun with *Power of Muzik* Songs

Read the lyrics and see if there are any that help you to express something that you have gone through.

Let this encourage you, in that other people have faced the same thing before. You are not the only person.

Share your troubles with people close to you.

Rehearsing at Paramount Pictures in Los Angeles

Fire (Power Of Music)
Luena Official and Big Zuu

It's the power of music
When you're lost, disillusioned
When you're caught in the fire

Help me out, I've been feeling something
Words won't come out but the feeling's sinking
I feel I'm sinking, yeah
Simmer down, got my favourite song
Take me away, where nobody else knows
Where nobody can go

I said it's okay to be up but then get down
Just play something when the words won't
When the words won't come out

It's the power of music
When you're lost, disillusioned
When you're caught in the fire
And a life's on the line

It's the sound of the broken
Giving hope to the hopeless
When you know how to use it
It's the power of music

Don't hold back, never run away
I've been on a road, going through the same thing
Been going through the same thing
This is the voice of the dreamers
Turn up the sound of the speakers
There's no discriminative feature
It just feels so good

I said it's okay to be up but then get down
Just play something when the words won't come out

It's the power of music
When you're lost, disillusioned
When you're caught in the fire
And a life's on the line
It's the sound of the broken
Giving hope to the hopeless
When you know how to use it
It's the power of music

When you're caught in the fire
When you're caught in the fire

Yeah, it's the power in the music
Make the people come in tune
Yeah, we know it's only sound but still
It's lighting up the room
Because it brings us all together
   when we're singing in a group

And still we're aiming for the top
We're going straight up through the roof
Yeah, I can't lie man I'm happy where it's taken me
I put my life in the lyrics I had to have the faith in me
But over time other people started rating me
Playing all my riddims and for the shows
    they started paying me
Yeah I'm happy how my journey's gone
I know people that learn my songs yeah
You can make it if you're working strong
Because we all got a story that's a worthy one
Be yourself don't have to follow the main crowd
As long you're making your family and mates proud
Cause we're all unique with a great sound
Power of the music yeah you know they won't take down
Yeah

It's the power of music
When you're lost, disillusioned
When you're caught in the fire
And a life's on the line
It's the sound of the broken
Giving hope to the hopeless
When you know how to use it
It's the power of music

Worth It
Luena

We've been here before
Neighbours banging on the walls
(Boy just let me speak)
You can walk away
Bet you gotta place to stay
(Damn you make me weak)

Yeah you really got me hurt
Saying those 3 little words
So if you mean it then
Won't you come and show me I'm your priority

Give and take it
Up and down again

Na na na
Boy you're worth the pain
You're worth it
(You're worth it)

When there's no pain
There ain't no gain
You're worth it
(You're worth it)

When you leave me
I want more
Back and forth in this love

Na na na
Boy you're worth the pain
You're worth it

Here we go again
Talking about me to your friends
(I'm not losing sleep)
Then you come around mine
Pretending you're fine
(Boy you're so deep)

When I reach out
You pull back
Too many times
I can't keep track

So if you're serious
Doesn't take a genius
(Boy just take the lead)

Give and take it
Up and down again

Shake
DJ Sonique, Wendy Sheppard, Reece, PoM singers

Follow us if you want to live
If you want to do more than just exist
There's a chemical feeling inside of our bodies
(Oh yeah yeah yeah)
Tellin' us to get wild tellin' us to get naughty
Alright alright

You better shake
Better shake what your mama made
Babe
Take it low till you ricochet
Hey
In the back of the Uber it's payday
So let the beat play
We're gonna work work work and we'll party all night
(Alright alright)
We're gonna make that money then we'll spend it right
But right now

You better shake
We're gonna move like there's nobody else around
We're gonna take the night
We're gonna shut it down
There's gon' be nothing but good vibes
Tonight
Wind to the beat jus' rock to the bass line
Shake your body like you're having a good time
Alright alright

There's a chemical feeling inside of our bodies
(Oh yeah yeah yeah)
Tellin' us to get wild tellin' us to get naughty
(Alright alright)
Cos tomorrow is promised to no-one
Live like it's the last one
Let me see you grab someone

And just shake
Shake what your mama made
Babe
Take it low till you ricochet
Hey
In the back of the Uber it's payday
So let the beat play
We're gonna work work work and we'll party all night
(Alright alright)
We're gonna make that money then we'll spend it right
But right now
You better shake

Hummunaa
Hummunaa
Hummunaa

Hey-yeah
Hummunaa
Hummunaa
Hummunaa
Hey-yeah

I don't need nobody
I just want to move my body
I don't need nobody
I just want to, I just want to
I don't need nobody
I just want to move my body
I don't need nobody, nobody

Bruised
Michael Rice, Asher Knight, Luena Martinez

Sometimes I think we need a referee
Cause I'm up against the ropes everyday
This isn't how love's supposed to be
And I don't wanna keep living this way

Don't wanna apologise, especially when I'm in the right, oh I,
Don't wanna play the good guy this time
When are you gonna realise

That I'm bruised
Black and blue from loving you
Yes, I'm bruised
From taking every hurt you threw
At me, at me

Sometimes I think I give you the best part of me
And all you do is throw it away
I feel like I'm in love with the enemy
I keep fighting the losing game

Don't wanna apologise especially when I'm in the right oh
Don't wanna play the good girl this time
When are you gonna realise

That I'm bruised
Black and blue from loving you
Yes, I'm bruised
From taking every hurt you threw
Yes, I'm bruised
Black and blue from loving you
Yes, I'm bruised
From taking every hurt you threw
At me

I gotta heal, cause I need to feel how to love again
Oh baby baby
And I gotta mend cause I can't pretend that I'm ok
When I'm dying inside
When I take the risk, you burned the bridge
Now there is no way back to where we used to be
To where we used to be

Cause I'm bruised
Black and blue from loving you
Yes, I'm bruised
From taking every hurt you threw
And I'm bruised
Yes yes yes
Black and blue from loving you
Yes, I'm bruised
From taking every hurt you threw
At me, at me, at me, at me, at me, at me
At me, at me
Oh at me

You
Denis Coleman

Sometimes you seem like a mystery
Seems like I'm seeing you in 2D
I'm only searching for answers
Yeah any answer you give to me

Do you believe in meant to be?
Cause I thought that it was meant to be
So much less of a hassle
Than this whole thing has been for me

But I don't want no drama
No negative karma
I just wanna take a ride
I just wanna take some time
I don't need a saga
Don't need all that gossip
I'm just curious no lie
Wanna get inside your mind

Tell me what you fall for
I just wanna know
Tell me what you stand for
Tell me what you love
Tell me what you're thinking
When I step in the room
Tell me who you think of when I say
You

Tell me who you think of when I say you

Tell me who you think of when I say you

Yeah every morning I think of you
(Think of you)
And I wanna know if you think about me too
If you could give me just one sign
If only you'd go and make a move
(Yeah)

But I don't want no drama
No negative karma
I just wanna take a ride
I just wanna take some time
I don't need a saga
Don't need all that gossip
I'm just curious no lie
Wanna get inside your mind

Tell me what you fall for
I just wanna know
Tell me what you stand for
Tell me what you love
Tell me what you're thinking
When I step in the room
Tell me who you think of when I say
You

Tell me who you think of when I say you

Tell me who you think of when I say you

Tell me who you think of
T-t-tell me who you think of
When I say

Tell me who you think of
T-t-tell me who you think of
When I say

I don't want no drama
No negative karma
I just wanna take a ride
I just wanna take some time
I don't need a saga
Don't need all that gossip
I'm just curious no lie
Wanna get inside your mind

Tell me what you fall for
I just wanna know
Tell me what you stand for
Tell me what you love
Tell me what you're thinking
When I step in the room
Tell me who you think of
When I say
You

About CeCe Sammy

Known as 'The UK's Vocal Whizz', CeCe Sammy is a leading vocal and performance coach who works in London and Los Angeles. She is known for her TV appearances, on screen and behind the scenes contributions as a vocal coach, TV judge, advisor, talent scout and trouble-shooter on various music and entertainment shows.

CeCe's successful career has led to her becoming the industry's go-to vocal and performance coach, as well as a major name in the global music industry. In 2016, CeCe was chosen to be the Chairperson of the UK Jury of Eurovision, the longest-running annual international TV song competition (and one of the most watched non-sporting events in the world!). Since 2017, CeCe has worked closely with the BBC, in part as Series Head Vocal Coach for BBC One's *Let's Sing and Dance for Comic Relief*, and also as a member of the development team creating the show *Pitch Battle*. She has most recently been Head Vocal Coach on the BBC's new singing show *All Together Now* and BBC show *This Is My Song*. CeCe has also been a member of the *BRIT Awards Voting Academy* since 2017.

CeCe's on- and off-screen credits are phenomenal, with her working on shows including *Pop Idol / American Idol, America's Got Talent, The X Factor, The Voice UK, Just The Two Of Us, E! Entertainment* and many more. She has also become a guest columnist for *OK! Magazine*, interviewing

CeCe Sammy

celebrities such as Billy Gibbons (ZZ Top), Colbie Caillat, Anthony Hamilton, Jazmine Sullivan, Randy Jackson, Estelle, Mary Mary, Black Eyed Peas, Eric Benet and Fantasia at events including the *Grammy Awards, American Music Awards* and more.

CeCe is also known for her voluntary work. She has been invited to 10 Downing Street on a number of occasions for Local Charity, *Speakers for Schools* and events for the *Department for Digital, Culture, Media & Sport.*

CeCe with The Chasers from ITV's The Chase *(Jenny Ryan, Mark Lebbett, Anne Hegerty and Shaun Wallace) when they won BBC's charity competition show,* Let's Sing and Dance

Thanks

Special Thanks to:

Isabella Francesca Seyara – my inspiration, my princess, my everything.

Anna Sammy – my mother and my hero!

Athena Sammy – my sister who will always be my best friend, my baby sister and my steadfast rock!

Thanks to key work colleagues

Terry Ronald, Jayne Collins & all the team at Cool Hand Media Group, Jamesy, Kwame Kwaten, Lew Parker, Kris Norvik and Jamie Skinner. To Malcolm Garrett (designer extraordinaire), Todd Swift and the Eyewear editing team.

To everyone I have ever vocal coached and who feature in this book from the UK and USA. Without you, I could never have written this book!

God Above!